Anand

THE CITY OF BLISS

MW00964179

Ph: 6540738, 2740738
Lahore Book Shop
Near Society Cinema,
LUDHIANA-141008,

Anandpur

THE CITY OF BLISS

Text by Mohinder Singh
Photographs by Sondeep Shankar

UBS PUBLISHERS' DISTRIBUTORS LTD.
IN ASSOCIATION WITH
NATIONAL INSTITUTE OF PANJAB STUDIES

NATIONAL INSTITUTE OF PANJAB STUDIES, NEW DELHI

Advisory Committee:

Prof. Mulk Raj Anand
Prof. Amrik Singh
Prof. Bipan Chandra
Dr. J.S. Neki
Prof. B.N. Goswamy

Series Editor: Dr. Mohinder Singh
Research Associate: Rishi Singh

UBS PUBLISHERS' DISTRIBUTORS LTD.

5 Ansari Road, New Delhi-110 002
Phones: 3273601, 3266646 • Cable: ALLBOOKS • Fax: 3276593, 3274261
E-mail: ubspd@gobookshopping.com • Website: www.gobookshopping.com

10 First Main Road, Gandhi Nagar, Bangalore-560 009
Phones: 2263901, 2263902, 2253903 • Cable: ALLBOOKS
Fax: 2263904 • E-mail: ubspd.bng@bgl.vsnl.net.in

6, Sivaganga Road, Nungambakkam, Chennai-600 034
Phones: 8276355, 8270189 • Cable: UBSIPUB • Fax: 8278920
E-mail: ubspd.che@md4.vsnl.net.in

8/1-B, Chowringhee Lane, Kolkata-700 016
Phones: 2441821, 2442910, 2449473 • Cable: UBSIPUBS
Fax: 2450027 • E-mail: ubspdcal@cal.vsnl.net.in

5 A, Rajendra Nagar, Patna-800 016
Phones: 672856, 673973, 686170 • Cable: UBSPUB • Fax: 686169
E-mail: ubspdpat@dte2.vsnl.net.in

80, Noronha Road, Cantonment, Kanpur-208 004
Phones: 369124, 362665, 357488 • Fax: 315122
E-mail: ubsknp@sancharnet.in

Distributors for Western India:
M/s Preface Books
Unit No. 223 (2nd floor), Cama Industrial Estate,
Sun Mill Compound, Lower Parel (W), Mumbai-400 013
Phone: 022-4988054 • Telefax: 022-4988048 • E-mail: Preface@vsnl.com

Overseas Contact:
475 North Circular Road, Neasden, London NW2 7QG, U.K.
Tele: (020) 8450-8667 • Fax: (020) 8452 6612 Attn: UBS

© National Institute of Panjab Studies

First Published 2002

First Reprint 2002

All rights reserved. No part of this publication may be reproduced or transmitted in any form or by any means, electronic or mechanical, including photocopying, recording, or any information storage or retrieval system, without prior permission in writing from the publisher.

Cover & Book Design: Dushyant Parasher

Processed and Printed by
Ajanta Offset & Packagings Ltd., New Delhi

Cover
Panoramic view of Takhat Kesgarh Sahib, Anandpur
Photo © Hardev Singh

Half title page
A Nihang in a state of bliss

Title spread
In preparation for the tercentenary celebrations of the Khalsa, the whole city of Anandpur was painted white.

Foreword

The National Institute of Panjab Studies was established in 1990 to promote research on different aspects of Panjabi life and letters. It was subsequently recognised by the Panjab University, Chandigarh, as an advanced centre of learning. Apart from promoting research, the Institute has also been organising lectures, seminars and conferences. Some conferences were also organised in collaboration with other institutions such as the Department of Multicultural Education, University of London, Department of South Asian Studies, University of Michigan, Ann Arbor and the Centre for Global Studies, University of California, Santa Barbara. To mark fifty years of India's independence, the Institute organised an international seminar on 'Partition in Retrospect' in collaboration with the India International Centre, New Delhi.

In connection with the tercentenary of the Khalsa in 1999, the Institute took up a major research project of locating and cataloguing relics which are popularly associated with the Sikh gurus and other historical personalities. Our research team led by the Director of the Institute, visited various parts of India and Pakistan, and located and listed a number of valuable relics. During their field work our team located some very precious relics such as the *chola* of Guru Nanak, the *chola* of Guru Hargobind, *chola*, *dastar* and other relics of Guru Gobind Singh and Mata Sahib Kaur, sword-belt, *godri* and flag of Maharaja Ranjit Singh. Our team was able to take pictures of these and other precious relics and record popular evidence connected with these objects. The team also discovered some rare *Guru Granth Birs*, *hukamnamas* and other historical documents and coins issued by Banda Singh Bahadur, Sikh chiefs, Maharaja Ranjit Singh and his generals.

With a view to sharing the results of our research with the larger audience and creating awareness for proper preservation of the endangered heritage of Panjab and conservation of the valuable relics, the Institute has decided to bring out a series of pictorial books under the 'Panjab Heritage Series'.

The Institute would like to record its gratitude to the Department of Culture, Government of India, for its initial grant for preparing a 'Catalogue of the Sikh Relics', to the Government of the National Capital of Delhi and the Delhi Sikh Gurdwara Management Committee for their financial support for publication of these books and to various institutions and individuals for allowing the Institute's team access to their rich collections. I would also like to thank my colleagues on the Governing Council and staff of the Institute without whose active cooperation it would not have been possible to bring out these volumes.

Manmohan Singh

President
National Institute of Panjab Studies
Bhai Vir Singh Marg
New Delhi - 110 001

5

Acknowledgements

The National Institute of Panjab Studies acknowledges its gratitude to the following for their contribution to the Panjab Heritage Series:

- The National Museum, New Delhi
- The National Archives of India, New Delhi
- The Panjab State Archives and the Panjab State Museum, Chandigarh, Patiala and Amritsar
- The Shiromani Gurdwara Prabandhak Committee, Amritsar, for permitting us to take photographs of the relics in the Toshakhana of the Golden Temple and sacred weapons at the Akal Takhat, Amritsar, Takhat Sri Kesgarh Sahib, Anandpur, Takhat Damdama Sahib, Talwandi Sabo
- Takhat Sri Patna Sahib, Bihar
- Takhat Sri Hazoor Sahib, Nanded
- The Sikh Regimental Centre, Ramgarh
- Capt. Amarinder Singh, New Moti Bagh Palace, Patiala
- The Bagrian family at Quila Bagrian
- The Sangha family of Drolli Bhai Ki
- Family of Mai Desan, Chak Fateh Singhwala
- Family of Bhai Rupa, Village Bhai Rupa, Dist. Bhatinda
- Family of Bhai Dalla, Talwandi Sabo, Dist. Bhatinda
- Mrs. Jyoti Rai, American Numismatic Society
- Dr. Jean Marie Lafont, French Embassy, New Delhi
- Gurdwara Sri Hemkunt Sahib Management Trust, Kanpur
- S. Bhajan Singh, Chairman, Singapore Sikh Education Foundation
- Department of Archeology and Museums, Government of Pakistan, for permission to take photographs of Relics of Maharaja Ranjit Singh and his family in Princess Bamba collection, Lahore Fort Museum, Lahore
- Hardev Singh, Raghu Rai, Ashok Dilwali, Gurmeet Thukral, Manohar Singh, Satpal Danish and Dushyant Parasher for allowing to use their pictures
- Dr S S Bhugra, Dr Susan Stronge, J D Dewan, Mrs Mohinder Singh, Ranjit Kaur and Ashwani Kumar for their input to the project
- Faqir Syed Saif-ud-Din, Fakir Khana Museum, Lahore
- Syed Afzal Haidar, Lahore
- The Victoria & Albert Museum, London.

Facing page
Beating the nagara *is an important part of the Sikh tradition*

Spread on pages 8-9
Takhat Kesgarh Sahib illuminated during the night

Spread on pages 10-11
Front view of Takhat Kesgarh Sahib

Spread on pages 12-13
A view of the mammoth march taken out during the tercentenary celebrations

Spread on pages 14-15
Finale of Hola Mahalla *in river Charan Ganga*

Above: Scenes from the Sikh history constructed during the tercentenary celebrations

Facing page: Ten Sikh gurus from a rare Janamsakhi *illustration.*
Courtesy: Prof. Pritam Singh, Patiala

ounded by Guru Nanak (1469-1539), Sikhism developed as a major movement for the establishment of an egalitarian order under the successive gurus. Guru Nanak preached strict monotheism and described the Creator as *Ikk* (One), without a second. Guru Nanak's philosophy of God is best described in the *Japji*, the primal creed of the Sikh faith. Contrary to the medieval Indian practice of denouncing the world for spiritual elevation, Guru Nanak believed that the world was worth living. "This world is the abode of God and the True One lives therein," said the guru. Guru Nanak believed that it was possible to live pure amidst the impurities of life.

> As the lotus liveth detached in waters, as the duck floateth carefree on the stream, so doth one cross the Sea of Existence, his mind attuned to the Word. One liveth detached, enshrining the One Lord in the mind, shorn of hope, living in the midst of hope.

The movement made rapid advances under the first five gurus because of various developmental schemes launched by them. Liberal policies of the contemporary Mughal Emperor, Akbar, who showed great reverence towards the new faith, provided congenial atmosphere for the development of Sikhism, which made a powerful appeal to the downtrodden sections of society. However, the developing Sikh fraternity got a major setback when Jahangir succeeded Akbar as the emperor in AD 1605. Some of the religious bigots among the Muslim clergy had been viewing the development of the Sikh faith with suspicion, and they found a sympathiser in the new emperor who, soon after his accession to the throne, made a major shift in the state's religious policy.

Development of the Sikh faith, with its distinct institutions, network of missionaries and regular flow of voluntary labour and cash contributions for the construction of new towns by the gurus, was viewed by the critics of the Sikh movement as development of 'a state within a state'. Increasingly alarmed at the growing popularity of Guru Arjan among the Hindus and Muslims, Emperor Jahangir ordered his officials to confiscate all properties of the guru and torture him to death.

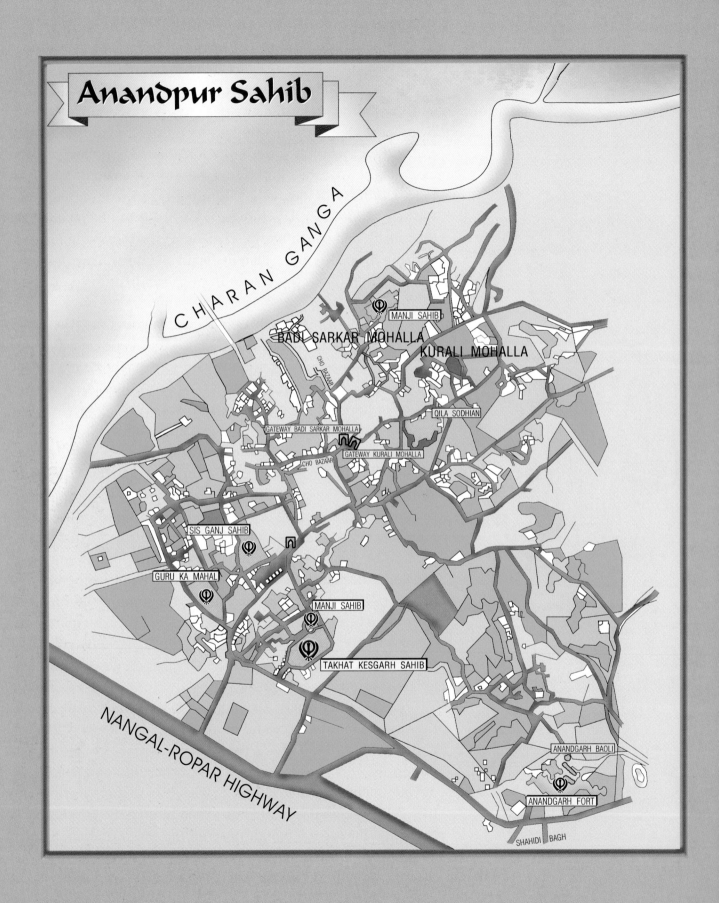

The martyrdom of Guru Arjan in AD 1606 was a turning point in Sikh history. His son and successor, Guru Hargobind, inaugurated a new policy of infusing martial spirit amongst the followers of the Sikh faith. In keeping with the parting message of Guru Arjan, "Let him sit fully armed on his throne and maintain an army to the best of his ability", Guru Hargobind wore two swords—*Miri* and *Piri*—symbolising a combination of temporal and spiritual authority. The guru also sent *hukamnamas* to the *masands* saying he would be pleased with those who brought him offerings of good horses and arms. Several young men flocked to the guru and he was able to raise an effective and strong body of troops ready to face any eventuality.

An important aspect of this new policy was the guru's decision to shift his headquarters from Amritsar to Kiratpur, a town on the outskirts of Anandpur Sahib. The guru's presence in the Malwa region and his focus on keeping arms encouraged the Jat peasantry of this region to join the Sikh movement.

Facing page: Map of Anandpur city

Below: Gurdwara Sheesh Mahal at Kiratpur emerged as an important centre of Sikh religio-political activities after Guru Hargobind shifted from Amritsar to this place.

Conversion of the Jat tribes of Malwa region of Panjab to Sikhism and their determination to fight Mughal oppression proved a turning point in Sikh history. It was from Kiratpur that Guru Hargobind sent preachers in different directions to broaden the base of the Sikh movement. Under the guru's direction his son, Baba Gurditta, appointed four preachers—Phul, Almast, Gonda and Balu Hasna—who founded four preaching centres called *dhuans* and spread the message of Sikhism far and wide. Some of the important hill chiefs such as those of Haripur, Kulu, Suket, Chamba, Kangra and Pilibhit, who were sympathetic to the Sikh religion, came closer to the guru.

The guru's visit to Bhatinda, Drolli Bhai Ki and other areas of

Facing page: Simarna *of Guru Hargobind*
Courtesy: Sangha family of Drolli Bhai Ki

Below: Gurdwara built in the memory of Guru Hargobind's eldest son Baba Gurditta

Left: Hukamnama *of Guru Hargobind*
Courtesy: Sangha family of Drolli Bhai Ki

Below: Gagar *of Guru Hargobind*
Courtesy: Sangha family of Drolli Bhai Ki

Far below: Tabalbaz *of Guru Hargobind*
Courtesy: Sangha family of Drolli Bhai Ki

Below right: Thals *of Guru Hargobind*
Courtesy: Sangha family of Drolli Bhai Ki

the Malwa belt of Panjab won him many new adherents, with some of the tribal chiefs embracing the Sikh faith. It was during the guru's visit to Malwa that Kala, ancestor of the ruling Phulkian family, along with his nephews, Sandli and Phul, visited the guru at Gurusar. According to popular tradition, Phul rubbed his belly when he felt hungry. When the guru asked why was the child behaving like this, Kala replied that he was very hungry, upon which the guru remarked: "What to talk of his hunger, his descendants will satisfy the hunger of millions. Their horses will drink water from Sutlej and Yamuna." The prophecy came true when Phul's descendants became rulers of the princely states of Patiala, Nabha and Jind. Tiloka and Rama, sons of Phul, greatly helped Guru Gobind Singh during his visit to Malwa. Pleased at their devotion, the tenth guru blessed them with a *hukamnama,* which described them as his favourite Sikhs and their house as guru's own. This *hukamnama* is still preserved with the descendants of the ruling family of Patiala.

Drolli Bhai Ki developed a special association with the house of the guru. While Guru Hargobind was busy fighting battles against the Mughals he left his wife, who was in advanced stage of pregnancy, in her sister's *haveli.* It was in this *haveli* that the guru's wife, Mata Damodri, gave birth to a son, Baba Gurditta. Guru Hargobind visited this village several

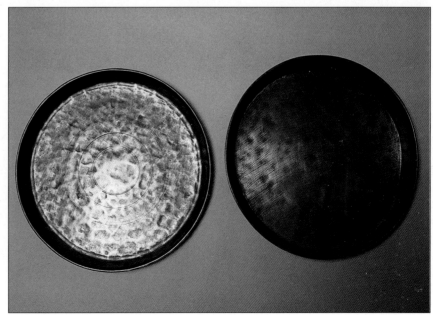

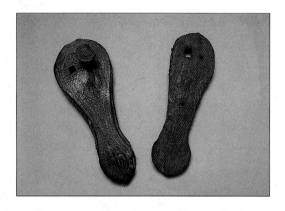

times and stayed in the *haveli* which has many precious relics, such as *kharawan, chola, thalis, gangasagar, tabalbaz* and *gagar* along with *hukamnamas*, preserved by the descendants of Bhai Sain Das. Guru's several victories against the Mughal rulers inspired the Jat peasantry and gave them a sense of self-confidence and pride as members of the new faith. They learnt for the first time that, given dynamic leadership and guidance, they had the potential to overthrow the tyrannical rulers who had been exploiting them for centuries. Awareness of their hidden potential by these new entrants in the Sikh movement proved a great asset for the Sikh gurus, especially Guru Gobind Singh who created the order of the Khalsa in AD 1699.

Above: Gangasagar *of Guru Hargobind*
Courtesy: Sangha family of Drolli Bhai Ki

Far above: Kharawan *of Guru Hargobind*
Courtesy: Sangha family of Drolli Bhai Ki

Right: Chola *of Guru Hargobind*
Courtesy: Sangha family of Drolli Bhai Ki

Facing page: Ancestors of the princely state of Patiala faithfully served the Sikh gurus and received special blessings in return. In the hukamnama *issued to Bhai Rama and Bhai Tiloka of the Phulkian states by Guru Gobind Singh, the guru described their house as his own. This* hukamnama *is preserved with the family.*
Courtesy: Captain Amarinder Singh

Following double spread: Kamarkasa of Guru Gobind Singh on which pauris *of Jaap Sahib are inscribed in gold*
Courtesy: Captain Amarinder Singh

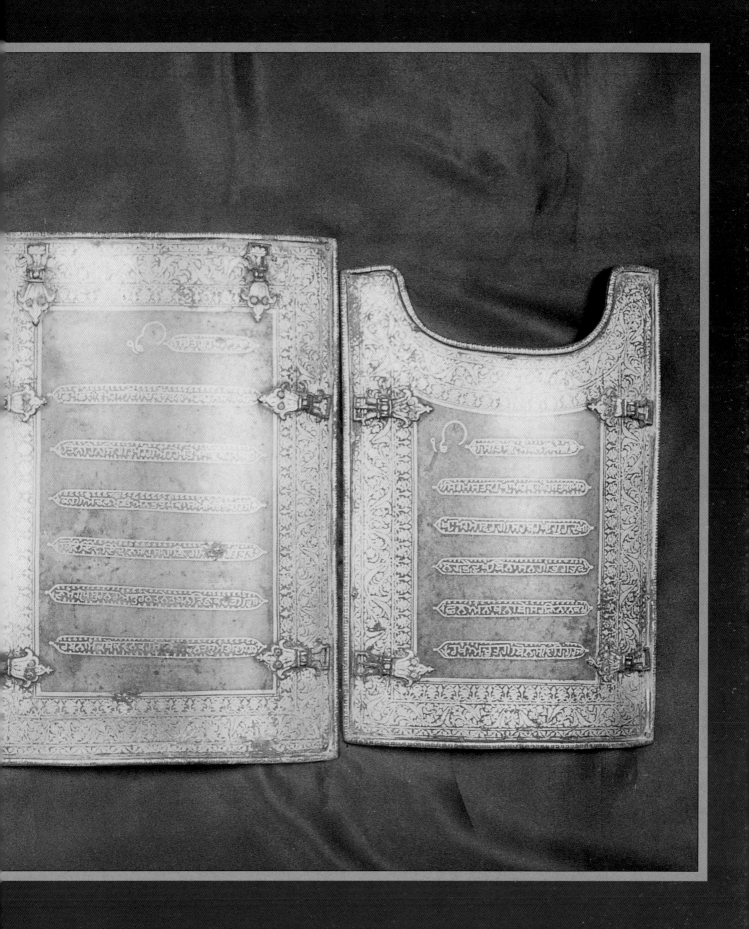

Guru Har Rai, who succeeded Guru Hargobind in AD 1644, continued the missionary activities in the Malwa region. It was because of the guru's tours in this area that many powerful chiefs came under the his influence. Another noticeable achievement of Guru Har Rai was the revival of the use of herbal medicines in and around Kiratpur. The guru not only encouraged his followers to pay special attention to the preservation of the natural environment around Kiratpur, which was conducive for the growth of medicinal herbs, but also started a *shafakhana* of herbal medicines. It is believed that Prince Dara Shikoh, son of Emperor Shah Jahan, was cured of a serious illness by the use of herbal medicines sent by the guru from his *shafakhana*. After recovery, the prince is believed to have visited Kiratpur to express his gratitude to the guru.

Aurangzeb, who succeeded Shah Jahan as the Emperor of India, did not like Guru Har Rai's friendship with Dara Shikoh, the defeated contestant to the throne. He summoned the guru to Delhi. Rather than going himself, the guru sent his elder son Ram Rai, to the emperor's court. Because of Ram Rai's misinterpretation of a hymn in the *Guru Granth* to please the emperor, the guru disowned him and instead appointed his younger son, Har Krishan, as his successor. Ram Rai did not take this kindly. With the help of some of the *masands*, Ram Rai declared himself as the guru and sought Emperor Aurangzeb's intervention to settle the issue in his favour. This resulted in the emperor calling Guru Har Krishan to Delhi.

During his stay in Delhi Guru Har Krishan fell seriously ill but, before leaving for his heavenly abode, he waved his hand in the air and, pointing out, said "Baba Bakale"—implying that the successor guru was to be found in the village of Bakala near Amritsar. Taking advantage of the situation, rival claimants —twenty two of them—installed themselves at Bakala, each one claiming to be the successor guru till a devout Sikh, Makhan Shah Lubana, was able to locate Tegh Bahadur, the youngest son of Guru Hargobind, who was lost in deep meditation in a cell. On hearing Makhan Shah's loud voice proclaiming *Guru ladho re* (I have found the real Guru), the Sikhs assembled there and installed Tegh Bahadur as the ninth guru with due ceremony.

Long absence of Guru Hargobind and his successors from Amritsar greatly emboldened the *masands* who had practically taken control of the Harimandir and adjoining gurdwaras. Rejected claimants to guruship, notably Dhir Mal and Ram Rai, also joined hands with these *masands* in their hostility towards Guru Tegh Bahadur. Dhir Mal even instigated a *masand* to make an attempt on the guru's life though he escaped the bullet attack. When, after a holy dip in the sacred tank, the guru wished to pay homage at the sanctum sanctorum in the Harimandir, the *masands* slammed the doors in his face. In such a hostile atmosphere at Amritsar, Guru Tegh Bahadur thought it prudent to move to Kiratpur along with his family. However, on reaching Kiratpur, the guru found that there too the jealousy of his collaterals plagued the place. Hence, he decided to establish a new town near Kiratpur called Chakk Nanaki, which later came to be known as Anandpur Sahib, the City of Bliss. The development of the new town was momentarily interrupted because of Guru Tegh Bahadur leaving on spiritual journeys to eastern India. However, with the return of the guru along with his family and young son, Gobind Rai, who was born in Patna, Anandpur Sahib fast developed as an important centre with devotees of the guru from different parts of India flocking the place. When the guru was busy in developing the town and propagating the message of the Sikh faith, a development took place at Anandpur Sahib which drastically changed the course of Sikh history.

Right: Gurdwara Guru de Mahal marks the place where foundation of Anandpur Sahib was laid. It was the residence of Guru Tegh Bahadur and Guru Gobind Singh for a number of years.

Religious intolerance of the Mughal rulers reached its peak when Aurangzeb became the Emperor of India. The Kashmiri Pandits became a special target of Aurangzeb's policy of persecution of non-Muslims. Driven to desperation, they decided to call upon Guru Tegh Bahadur at Anandpur Sahib to narrate their tale of woe and seek his intervention. As the guru was listening to their story, his young son, Gobind Rai, asked why he was so deeply preoccupied. The guru is said to have replied: "Grave are the burdens the earth carries. It will be redeemed only if a truly worthy person comes forward to offer his head." Young Gobind Rai spontaneously replied, "Father, none could be worthier than you for such a noble cause."

Guru Tegh Bahadur was pleased to hear the brave answer and resolved to court martyrdom to save the honour of those who looked up to him as their saviour. He told the Brahmins

Facing page: Historic Manji Sahib building

Below: Painting depicting the sis of Guru Tegh Bahadur being brought to Anandpur in a palanquin

that they should go back to Kashmir and tell the Mughal governor to inform Emperor Aurangzeb that if he was able to convert Guru Tegh Bahadur to Islam the Kashmiri Pandits would follow suit. On noticing the guru's defence of Kashmiri Pandits, orders were issued by the emperor for the guru's arrest and his attendance at the imperial court in Delhi. According to popular accounts, rather than being arrested at Anandpur Sahib, the guru volunteered to reach Delhi and was beheaded under a *banyan* tree in Chandni Chowk in Delhi on 11 November 1675, where now stands the historic Sis Ganj Gurdwara.

Guru Tegh Bahadur's martyrdom proved yet another turning point in Sikh history. His young son and successor, Gobind Rai, decided to prepare the community of followers to face the oncoming challenge and created the order of the Khalsa to defend righteousness and chastise the evil-doers.

Gurdwara Bibangarh marks the place where Guru Gobind Singh received the sis of his father, Guru Tegh Bahadur.

Right: Gurdwara built in the memory of the Bhai Jaita, later renamed Bhai Jeewan Singh

Below: Gurdwara Sis Ganj, Anandpur Sahib

Following double spread: Sunset at Gurdwara Thara Sahib

Double spread pages 36-37: Gurdwara Sis Ganj, Anandpur Sahib

Page 38: A beautiful mural in Gurdwara Sis Ganj, Anandpur Sahib

Page 39: Fresco work in Gurdwara Sis Ganj, Anandpur Sahib

Above: Gurdwara Bhangani Sahib where Guru Gobind Singh fought and won his first battle against the hill chiefs

Far above: Situated on the bank of Yamuna, Gurdwara Paonta Sahib marks the centre of literary activities of Guru Gobind Singh.

Facing page: Gate to Kurali Mohalla

On 17th December 1675, young Gobind Rai was proclaimed the tenth guru of the Sikhs. The first thing that he ordered on being installed as the guru was to prepare a big drum which he named *Ranjit Nagara*, meaning the drum that would bring victory in the battlefield. Since horse riding, wearing of arms and beating of drums were considered emblems of royalty, this created jealousy among the neighbouring hill chiefs. Raja Bhim Chand of Bilaspur was specially upset when, during one of his visits to the guru at Anandpur Sahib, he found that, apart from many unique and valuable things, the young guru also possessed a *prasadi hathi* which had been presented by Raja Rattan Rai of Assam as a token of friendship.

Raja Medni Parkash of Sirmur greatly admired Guru Gobind Rai and invited him to spend some time with him at Nahan as a royal guest. On arrival at Nahan, the guru and his family were given a warm welcome. The guru was also allowed to build a small fort at Paonta Sahib, not very far from Nahan. The guru was greatly fascinated by the serene setting of Paonta located on the bank of the river Yamuna and made it the centre of his literary activities. It was here that the guru composed poetry along with fifty-two poets in his court. After some time the guru returned to Anandpur Sahib.

It was from the historic town of Anandpur Sahib that Guru Gobind Singh fought many battles and broadened the base of his struggle before creating the Khalsa. The hostility between the Sikhs and Emperor Aurangzeb did not end with the martyrdom of Guru Tegh Bahadur. The neighbouring hill chiefs were also not very happy over Anandpur Sahib becoming an important centre of political activities of the Sikhs. The young guru had to carefully plan a strategy to win over the neighbouring chiefs and forge a common front against the oppressive officials of the Mughal emperor.

Logically, the Hindu states of Kangra hills should have been partners of the guru in his fight against the armies of the Mughal emperor. However, this did not happen because of two reasons—first, the jealousy of the hill chiefs over the growing popularity and military strength of the guru, and second, the hill chiefs' fear of inviting the wrath of the Mughal army in case

of an open alliance with the guru. In a situation like this, the guru had to be extra cautious and, at one stage, even faced the combined army of the hill chiefs in the battle of Bhangani. It was the first battle in which Guru Gobind Singh demonstrated his skill in warfare and was able to defeat the combined forces of the hill chiefs. The guru's victory in the battle of Bhangani proved a turning point in his future military campaigns. Many of the hill chiefs thought it prudent to join hands with the guru and face the Mughal army jointly in case of any future invasion by Aurangzeb's forces.

After establishing his supremacy in the first ever military campaign in Bhangani, the guru returned to Anandpur Sahib. To prepare his army to face the mighty Mughal empire, the guru evolved a carefully thought out military strategy, which included building of forts around the city of Anandpur Sahib, digging *baolis* for regular supply of drinking water, storing ration for the army, recruiting more and more young men in his army and training them in guerrilla warfare. It was at Anandpur Sahib that he created a special squad called *Nihangs*,

Left: Residences and markets were built on both sides of the rivulet called Cho *in Anandpur which has dried up. The place is now known as* Cho Bazaar

Below: A historic building in Anandpur city

Following double spread: Nihangs playing with colours during Hola Mahalla

43

Right: Nihangs in their colourful dresses

Facing page top: Langar being prepared and served by the Nihangs

Facing page below: Nihangs busy preparing sukh nidhan

Following double spread: Horses and Nihangs are inseparable.

Page 50: Hola Mahalla is the biggest annual event in Anandpur Sahib when devotees from all over the world march to the city

Page 51: A Nihang proudly displays his typical turban in the Hola Mahalla at Anandpur Sahib.

who were unlike the mercenaries recruited for warfare and were prepared to die at the call of the guru.

When the hill chiefs learnt that Emperor Aurangzeb was busy in the Deccan, they stopped paying tribute to his officials and made friendship with the guru. The matter was reported to the emperor, who at once sent his forces under Mian Khan to collect the tribute from the hill chiefs. A fierce battle was fought by the Mughal forces and the hill chiefs backed by the guru at Nadaun on the banks of river Beas and the Mughal forces were defeated. Greatly upset at this defeat, Aurangzeb sent imperial forces under his elder son, Prince Muazzim. However, due to intervention of Nand Lal Goya, a poet in the Mughal court but an admirer and a devotee of the guru, a clash was averted.

After the above incident the neighbouring hill chiefs accepted the supremacy of the guru. When the emperor was busy in his military campaigns in South India, his local officials did not think it prudent to challenge the guru's authority. Consequently, there was a period of peace in Anandpur Sahib with young Gobind Rai in full command of the situation. It was during this period that the guru made a deep study of the martial tradition and literature with a view to enthusing a new spirit among the people of India. It seems that before creating the order of the Khalsa, the guru wrote and popularised literature which appealed to the martial instincts of the native people. The fact that when he gave a call to volunteer heads for the cause men from places so far away as Bidar in Karnataka and Jagannath Puri in Orissa readily responded to his call shows that the message of the guru and his heroic deeds had travelled to almost all parts of the country by word of mouth.

Creation of the Khalsa

The most significant event that happened at Anandpur Sahib was the creation of the Khalsa, which not only transformed the Sikhs from sparrows to hawks but also brought this holy city of Anandpur Sahib on the world map. When the guru was convinced that the time was right to create a dedicated band of soldiers to defend *dharma*, he gave a call on the Baisakhi day of AD 1699, which happened to be 30th March that year. The guru appeared before the gathering in a rather dramatic manner.

Left: Guru Gobind Singh preparing khande ki pahul *and his wife, Mata Sahib Kaur, adding* patasas *in the baptismal* amrit *to be administered to* Panj Piaras *chosen for the purpose*

Carrying an unsheathed sword in his hand, the guru asked the audience: "Is there a Sikh who is prepared to offer his head to the guru as a sacrifice." There was complete silence and the atmosphere was charged with sensation. When the guru repeated the call, Daya Ram, a Sobti Khatri of Lahore, came forward to offer his head. The guru took him to a nearby enclosure. He returned with the sword dripping with blood and asked for another head. At this, Dharam Das, a Jat from Hastinapur, came forward and was similarly taken to the enclosure. When the guru asked for more heads, Mohkam Chand, a washerman from Dwarka, Himat Rai, a water-carrier from Jagannath Puri, and Sahib Chand, a barber from Bidar (Karnataka), came forward and were taken inside the enclosure.

To the utter surprise of the assembled audience, the guru came back with all the five Sikhs dressed alike with saffron clothes and neatly tied turbans, carrying *kirpans* and other symbols prescribed by the guru. The guru made a departure

Left: The historic khanda *associated with the amrit ceremony of* AD *1699.*

Below: Amrit *being prepared by the* Panj Piaras

from the earlier tradition of *charan pahul* and offered these five Sikhs *khande ki pahul*. He also gave them the surname of *Singh*, meaning lion, and called them *Panj Piaras*—the Five Beloved Ones. By making all of them drink *pahul* from the same bowl, the guru abolished the distinction of high and low based on the traditional caste system. The guru also set a unique tradition of equality by himself taking *pahul* from the five beloved ones, and from Gobind Rai he became Gobind Singh. The guru declared that he had passed on all the authority to the newly created order of the Khalsa.

Left: Amrit *being administered to the* sangat *at Takhat Kesgarh Sahib*

Below: Sikh women being administered baptismal amrit

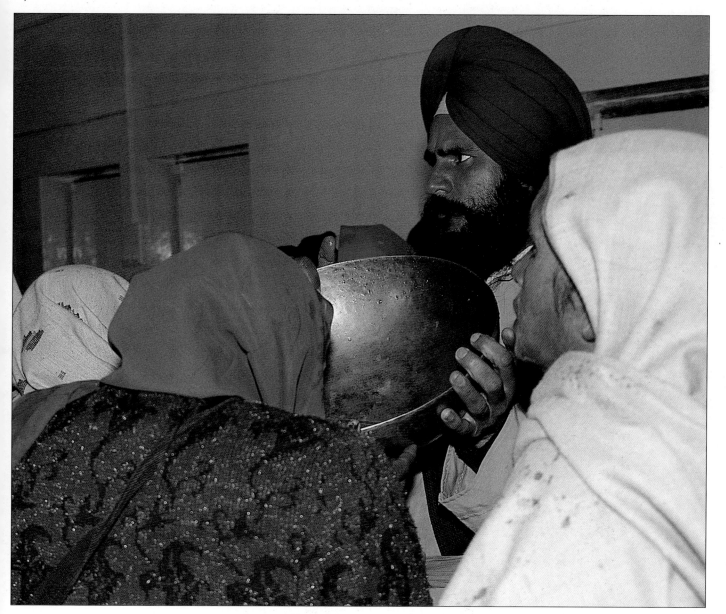

57

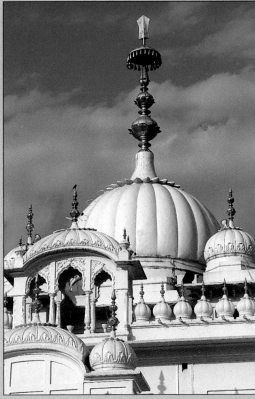

Above: Khanda *on the dome of Takhat Kesgarh Sahib*

Left: Panj Piaras *during the launching of the tercentenary celebrations*

Following double spread: An aerial view of Takhat Kesgarh Sahib and adjoining gurdwaras
Photo © Hardev Singh

Double spread pages 62-63: Sarovar of Takhat Kesgarh Sahib
Photo © Ashok Dilwali

Double spread pages 64-65: Takhat Kesgarh Sahib illuminated during the night

Double spread pages 66-67: Anandgarh Fort illuminated during the night

Creation of a casteless society and the fact that people from all corners of India had responded to the guru's call greatly alarmed the caste-conscious Rajput chiefs of the Shivalik hills near Anandpur Sahib. They approached the Raja of Bilaspur to evict the guru from Anandpur Sahib, which was located in his jurisdiction. When their repeated attacks failed to deter the guru, they collectively approached Emperor Aurangzeb for help. The guru, who was conscious that one day he would have to face a combined attack from the hill chiefs and the Mughal forces, had prepared himself well. A fierce battle followed at Anandpur and the combined forces of the Mughals and the Rajput chiefs were not able to defeat the guru's forces entrenched at Anandgarh. After months of siege, the Mughal commanders entered into negotiations with the guru. The guru and the soldiers were promised a safe escape in case they vacated Anandpur Sahib. However, when they came out of the fort, the Mughal armies betrayed the guru and many of his soldiers were killed; but the guru escaped safely to the Malwa region with the help of two Muslim devotees, Ghani Khan and Nabi Khan.

A group of visitors praying at Gurdwara Anandgarh

After Guru Gobind Singh's departure from Anandpur the town and its surrounding areas were badly damaged by the invading Mughal forces and the neighbouring hill chiefs. Anandgarh and other forts were destroyed. To avoid persecution at the hands of the oppressive invading armies most of the inhabitants, including the Sodhi families, also left the town. As a result, the historic gurdwaras, *baolis* and *havelis* became victims of neglect. It was during the rise of Sikh *misls* to political power that attention was paid by the Sikh chiefs towards locating, repairing or building historic Sikh shrines throughout Panjab and Delhi. Sardar Baghel Singh, one of the Sikh chiefs, paid special attention to the gurdwaras in Anandpur Sahib and nearby towns of Kiratpur, Paonta and Bhangani. He got some of the old forts and gurdwaras repaired and made provisions for carrying on regular service and recitation of *gurbani* and *langar* arrangements in Kesgarh. Like other historic Sikh shrines the control of most of the gurdwaras in Anandpur Sahib was either in the hands of the Sodhi chiefs or the Udasi *mahants*. It was the Gurdwara Reform Movement of 1920-25 which brought these gurdwaras under the control of the Shiromani Gurdwara Prabhandak Committee.

Fort of Sodhis in a dilapidated condition

While transfer of control of the gurdwaras from the hands of hereditary *mahants* to the Shiromani Gurdwara Prabhandak Committee put an end to the mismanagement, it has introduced certain new elements which are not conducive to the preservation of historic monuments and relics associated with the Sikh gurus. In their overenthusiasm some of those put in charge of the *kar-seva* of the historic gurdwaras are fast demolishing historic buildings and creating huge marble structures which have no historic and cultural importance. In order to build a wide road, the historic hill from where Guru Gobind Singh created the Khalsa in AD 1699 was levelled to the ground. Steps of the historic *baoli* of Anandgarh fort made of old bricks which were sanctified by the touch of Guru Gobind Singh's feet have been covered with marble slabs. Some of the old *havelis* and forts have almost disappeared while others are facing serious threat of extinction because of neglect and

Left: An old building in the city

Below: An old historic building associated with Bhai Nand Lal, poet laureate of Guru Gobind Singh

Following page: The historic baoli *of Bhai Kanahiya in village Mohival*

Page 73 top: The historic baoli *of Anandgarh Fort*

Page 73 below: Back wall of the haveli *of Sodhis near Bhora Sahib*

ignorance of their rich heritage. Because of the economic backwardness of the area coupled with the fact that Anandpur is not on the main railway track or highway, the town attracts large number of devotees only during special festive occasions such as Hola Mahalla and Baisakhi. During the tercentenary of the Khalsa in AD 1999 the Government of Panjab took several measures to restore the old glory of the historic town, including widening of roads and painting the whole town white. Unfortunately not much attention has been paid towards the conservation of a large number of old buildings, *havelis*, gates and bazaars which have great historic importance. During a survey of the area on the outskirts of Anandpur we found remnants of a number of forts which had been built by the guru for the defence of Anandpur but are not recorded anywhere. There is a need to make serious and conserted effort to preserve the rich heritage of Anandpur Sahib in view of town's importance in Sikh history.

Above: Ardas *being offered before display of relics at the Takhat*

Far above: Takhat Kesgarh Sahib

Facing page left: The historic saif *belonging to Hazrat Ali, son-in-law of Prophet Mohammed*

Facing page right: Bandook *of Guru Gobind Singh*

Following are some of the important forts and gurdwaras in Anandpur Sahib.

Takhat Sri Kesgarh Sahib

Takhat Sri Kesgarh marks the place where Guru Gobind Singh created the order of the Khalsa on the Baisakhi of AD 1699. It is one of the five *takhats*—seats of temporal authority of the Sikh *panth*—and the principal shrine at Anandpur Sahib. The *takhat* is situated on a small mountain in the east of the town. After the departure of the guru from Anandpur Sahib in AD 1705, the *takhat*, along with other gurdwaras, remained neglected. It was during AD 1936-44 that the present three-storeyed structure was constructed at the place where the Khalsa was created. The 16-meter square hall with balcony in front contains the sanctum sanctorum in which weapons and other relics of Guru Gobind Singh are preserved and are displayed every evening. On the top storey is the place where *amrit* is administered to the devotees. Recently the *takhat* and other adjoining gurdwaras were given a new look. While doing the renovations of this building, the old historic doors of the upper storey have been preserved intact. The following important relics popularly associated with Guru Gobind Singh, Bhai Bachitar Singh and Hazrat Ali, son-in-law of Prophet Mohammed, are preserved in Takhat Sri Kesgarh Sahib.

Khanda

According to popular accounts, it is the same historic *khanda* with which the tenth guru prepared *khande ki pahul* and administered it to the *panj piaras*. This *khanda* was once taken to the Akal Takhat in AD 1982 and *amrit* was prepared with it and administered to the *sangat*. Keeping in mind the historic value of the *khanda*, it was not allowed to be taken out of Kesgarh Sahib thereafter.

Katar

This historic dagger was a part of Guru Gobind Singh's *kamarkasa*. The guru used this weapon in hand-to-hand fight.

Saif

According to popular accounts, Mughal Emperor Bahadur Shah presented this *saif* (double-edged sword), to Guru Gobind Singh.

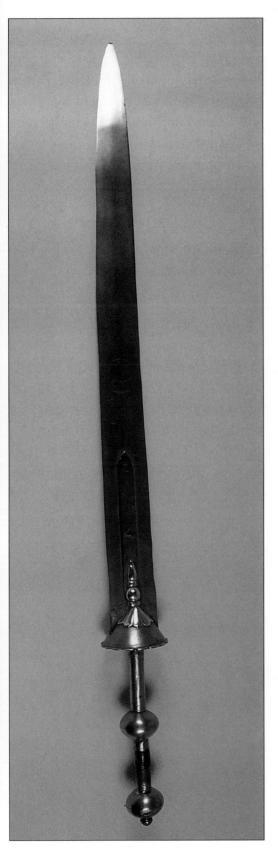

It is believed that this sword belonged to Prophet Muhammed's son-in-law, Hazrat Ali. The Prophet's grandsons, Hasan and Hussain, also used this weapon. Thereafter, this sword remained with the Islamic *khalifas* who gifted it to Emperor Aurangzeb. From Aurangzeb, this sword came to his son Bahadur Shah who presented it to Guru Gobind Singh because of guru's help in the war of succession.

Bandook

A Sikh follower from Lahore presented this *bandook* (gun) to Guru Gobind Singh. After the martyrdom of Guru Teg Bahadur, Guru Gobind Singh sent *hukamnamas* to the sikhs that whenever they come to Anandpur Sahib they should bring good horses and weapons as presents. As a result, many weapons, including this *bandook*, were presented to the *guru* by the visiting *sangat*.

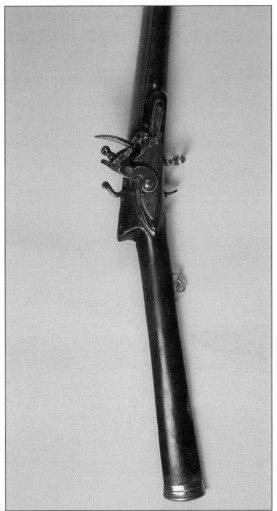

Nagini Barcha

This spear looks like a snake. That is why it is known as *nagini barcha*. A blow of this weapon was so strong that the victim could hardly survive. This was the personal *barcha* of the guru. In September AD 1700, Ajmer Chand and other hill chiefs came to attack Anandpur Sahib. A drunken elephant led their army. The elephant's head was protected by iron shields. The guru sent Bhai Bachitar Singh with this *nagini barcha*. Bhai Bachitar Singh came near the gate of Lohgarh and attacked the drunken elephant with this *barcha*. The *barcha* struck at the forehead of the elephant. In panic, the elephant went berserk and, while retreating, trampled many of the attacking army.

Karpa Barcha

It is in the shape of a hand, therefore it is called *karpa barcha*. It was only used during historical moments. In the year AD 1673 when the guru was engaged to Mata Jito ji, the guru's father-in-law wanted the marriage party to go to Lahore. However, instead of going to Lahore, the guru established a new township near Anandpur Sahib and named it Guru ka Lahore. When people complained of water shortage, the guru struck the ground with this very *barcha* three times and water came out gushing.

Facing page: Nagini barcha *of Guru Gobind Singh*

Below: Karpa barcha *of Guru Gobind Singh*

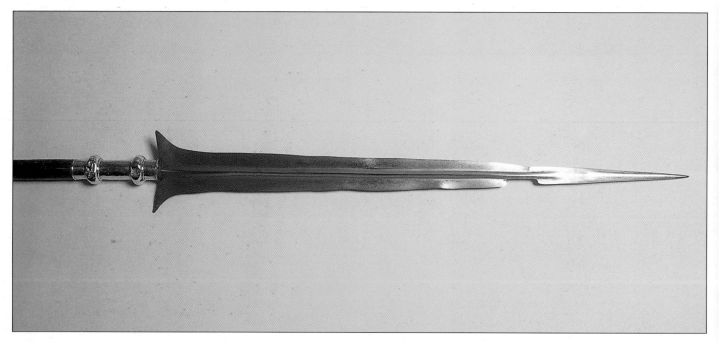

Relics of Guru Gobind Singh brought from England in AD 1966

Some historic relics of Guru Gobind Singh, which were taken to England after the annexation of Maharaja Ranjit Singh's kingdom by the British in AD 1849, were returned to India in AD 1966 to mark the tercentenary of the birth of Guru Gobind Singh. These are now preserved at Takhat Kesgarh along with the other weapons. These are: (i) *shamsheer wa sipur* (a sword and shield), (ii) *shamsheer tegha* (a scimitar), (iii) *dah-e-ahini* (an iron weapon), (iv) *neza* (a lance), (v) *burchee* (a small spear) and (vi) *burcha* (a long spear).

On the upper storey of Takhat Kesgarh Sahib, historic relics, including those of Guru Gobind Singh, are preserved and displayed to the sangat *every evening*

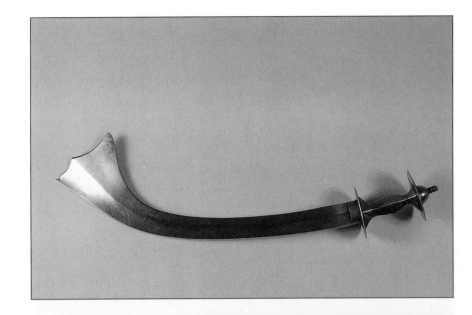

Right: Shamsheer-e-Tegha, *scimitar of Guru Gobind Singh*

Right below: Dhal *made of hippopotamus skin used by Guru Gobind Singh*

Below: Dah-e-ahini *of Guru Gobind Singh*

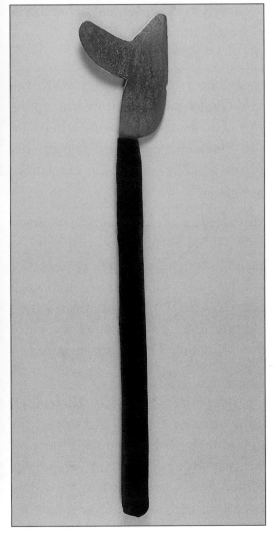

Above: Manji Sahib, Anandpur

Far above: Gurdwara Sis Ganj, Anandpur

Right top: Gurdwara Dumalgarh, Anandpur

Right below: Gurdwara built in the memory of Guru Gobind Singh's wife, Mata Jito ji, on the outskirts of the city

Gurdwara Guru de Mahal

This complex comprises gurdwaras Bhora Sahib, Manji Sahib and Damdama Sahib. It was at this place where the foundation of the new town Chakk Nanaki (later Anandpur Sahib) was laid by building Guru de Mahal, the personal residence of Guru Tegh Bahadur and later Guru Gobind Singh. Four sons of Guru Gobind Singh—Sahibzadas Ajit Singh, Jujhar Singh, Zoravar Singh and Fateh Singh—were born and brought up here. The other gurdwaras and forts in the complex are briefly listed in what follows.

Gurdwara Bhora Sahib

This gurdwara marks the site where Guru Tegh Bahadur used to sit in meditation in this *bhora*. He also composed his hymns here. Bhora Sahib is still preserved in the basement of the three-storeyed domed building raised later.

Gurdwara Manji Sahib

This part of the complex was known as *Diwan-e-Aam*. It was here that the ninth guru held congregations and instructed his followers in the use of arms. This is also the place where the Kashmiri Pandits came to meet the guru and sought his intervention to save them from forcible conversion to Islam.

Gurdwara Damdama Sahib

This gurdwara was the *Diwan-e-Khas* of Guru Tegh Bahadur. It is also known as Gurdwara Takhat Sahib. The guru used to hold his court here and perform functions which were earlier performed from the Akal Takhat. Adjacent to Gurdwara Damdama Sahib is a platform, called Thara Sahib, from where the guru addressed large gatherings. It also marks the place where Guru Gobind Singh was installed as the tenth guru.

Gurdwara Sis Ganj

Guru Tegh Bahadur was martyred in Delhi on 11 November, 1675. The severed head of the guru was brought to Anandpur Sahib by a devout Sikh, Bhai Jaita, and was cremated there on 17 November, 1675. When Guru Gobind Singh left Anandpur Sahib in AD 1705, he appointed Bhai Gurbaksh Das, an Udasi Sikh, as incharge of the place and instructed him to look after the shrine.

Gurdwara Akal Bunga

Opposite Gurdwara Sis Ganj is situated Gurdwara Akal Bunga marked by a raised platform. It is the place from where Guru Gobind Singh addressed the Sikhs gathered at the time of the cremation of Guru Tegh Bahadur and advised them to live according to the will of the Almighty.

Gurdwara Dumalgarh Sahib

This gurdwara lies on the northern side of Kesgarh Sahib. It is the place where Guru Gobind Singh used to train his sons in the art of warfare. It was also used as a playground. The story behind the name of this place goes back to November, 1703, when Ajmer Chand, the ruler of Bilaspur, attacked Anandpur Sahib. During the battle, the Khalsa flag was damaged. When it was reported to Guru Gobind Singh, he tore a small piece of cloth (*farra*) from his under turban (*keski*) and then set it in his turban in the form of a hanging flag called *dumala*. Guru Gobind Singh declared at that time that in future the Khalsa flag will be a part of the turban of every Sikh. Guru's son, Sahibzada Fateh Singh, only five years old at that time, also hung a *farra* in his turban as instructed by the guru. Therefore, the gurdwara came to be known as Gurdwara Dumalgarh.

Gurdwara Shahidi Bagh

A number of Sikhs sacrificed their lives when the army of Raja of Bilaspur laid siege to Anandpur Sahib in AD 1705. This gurdwara was built to commemorate their sacrifice and is named Shahidi Bagh.

Gurdwara Mata Jito ji

Guru Gobind Singh's first wife, Mata Jito ji, who died on 5 December, 1700, was cremated at this place in the outskirts of Anandpur Sahib. The gurdwara was built in her memory.

Quila Anandgarh

This fort, situated about three kilometers to the south of Anandpur Sahib, is on top of another hillock. The foundation stone of this fort was laid on 31 March, 1689 and it was the first fort of Anandpur Sahib built by Guru Gobind Singh to meet the requirements of war against the Mughals and their hill allies. Guru Gobind Singh spent about sixteen years in this fort. When he left Anandpur Sahib in December 1705, he began his journey from this fort. It was also used as a storehouse of arms and ammunitions of the Khalsa army and was of immense importance from military point of view.

This fort was attacked by Raja Ajmer Chand in December 1705 and was almost demolished by his army. During the 1960s the Sikhs built a gurdwara at the site of Anandgarh fort with a square domed sanctum in the middle of a square hall under the supervision of Sant Seva Singh. There is also a wide well, called Baoli Sahib, which is situated on the lower level of the hill.

Till 1985, some traces of the old building could be seen but, after the construction of a new building on the northern side of the fort, the signs of the old structure have completely disappeared.

Gurdwara Holgarh

One-and-a-half kilometer north-west of the town across Charan Ganga, Gurdwara Holgarh marks the place where Guru Gobind Singh started the practice of celebrating Hola Mahalla in AD 1701. Celebrated a day after the Hindu festival of Holi, Hola Mahalla is celebrated when Nihangs, knight-errants of Guru Gobind Singh, display their martial arts amidst sprinkling of colours. This is the biggest annual festival of Anandpur Sahib when bands of Nihangs from all over the country descend on the town in preparation for the event. The march starts from the open ground of Holgarh when sports like fencing, quoit-throwing and tent-pegging are held, apart from horse-riding and display of martial arts by the Nihangs with thousands of spectators from all over the world watching the finale at the Charan Ganga rivulet.

Quila Lohgarh

One-and-a-half kilometer south-west of Takhat Kesgarh Sahib, this is second strongest fort in Anandpur Sahib. *Lohgarh* literally means 'the iron-fort'. Guru Gobind Singh built it for the defence of Anandpur Sahib. The guru had also set up a factory for manufacturing arms in this fort. This is also the place where Bhai Bachitar Singh killed a drunken elephant let loose by the enemy camp by piercing a spear in the forehead of the elephant.

Below: Gurdwara Anandgarh, Anandpur

Far below: Gurdwara Holgarh, Anandpur

Facing page top: Gurdwara Fatehgarh Sahib, Anandpur

Facing page middle: Gurdwara Guru ka Lahore

Facing page below: Gurdwara Tribeni Sahib

Quila Fatehgarh

This fort, on the northern outskirts of the town, was built in the territory of village Sahota to defend the town of Chakk Nanaki, later Anandpur Sahib. The present double-storeyed domed structure was constructed during the 1980s.

Baoli of Bhai Kanehiya

The historic *baoli* from where Bhai Kanahiya used to carry water for serving the wounded soldiers in the guru's camp as well as those of the enemy is located at the outskirts of the town. The old *baoli* with stone linings is still intact. The Government of Panjab has declared this *baoli* along with the adjoining village Mohival as the Heritage Village.

Gurdwaras of Guru ka Lahore

In AD 1685 Gobind Rai's marriage was arranged with Bibi Sundri, daughter of Bhai Bhikan of Lahore. The bride's father insisted that the guru should go to Lahore along with marriage procession. Because of hostilities with the Mughal authorities, the guru thought it expedient to have the marriage ceremony performed near Anandpur Sahib and created a new township on the outskirts, which came to be popularly called Guru ka Lahore. It is eleven kilometers from Anandpur Sahib. The gurdwaras that commemorate the event are: (i) Gurdwara Tribeni Sahib, the place where the guru created a stream of water by piercing the ground with *karpa barcha*, (ii) Gurdwara Paur Sahib, (iii) Gurdwara Sehra Sahib and (iv) Gurdwara Anand Karaj (where the marriage ceremonies were performed).

Gurdwaras at Kiratpur Sahib

On the Chandigarh-Ropar road, there is the big establishment of Kiratpur. Baba Sri Chand, son of Guru Nanak, laid the foundation of Kiratpur in AD 1624 by starting work on a *baoli* and included four villages of Jiowal, Kalianpur, Bhatoli and Bhagowal. Guru Hargobind came here in AD 1635 and made the place his headquarters for some time. The seventh and the eighth gurus were born here. Guru Tegh Bahadur also lived here. Guru Gobind Singh visited this place a number of times. During his *udasis*, Guru Nanak also halted here. At this place there are sites associated with six gurus. There are sites associated with Baba Sri Chand, Baba Gurditta (son of Guru Hargobind) and Bibi Rup Kaur (daughter of Guru Har Rai).

Gurdwara Charan Kamal

Gurdwara Charan Kamal, Kiratpur

This gurdwara was built in the memory of Guru Nanak Dev. During his *udasis,* Guru Nanak halted here along with Bhai Mardana. As soon as a local Muslim saint, Budhan Shah, came to know about the arrival of the guru, he went to offer milk to him. The *takia* of Budhan Shah is built on a hilltop not far from the gurdwara.

Gurdwara Sheesh Mahal

After laying the foundation of Kiratpur in AD 1624, this was the first building that was constructed here. After shifting to Kiratpur, Guru Hargobind stayed here. Guru Har Rai, Guru Har Krishan, Ram Rai and Bibi Rup Kaur (son and daughter of Guru Har Rai) were born here.

Gurdwara Takhat Sahib

After shifting to Kiratpur, Guru Hargobind established his headquarters here and constructed a *takhat* like the Akal Takhat. At this place, Guru Har Rai and Guru Har Krishan were given their guruship.

Gurdwara Damdama Sahib

At this place Guru Har Rai used to meet the *sangat* which came from far and near.

Gurdwara Harimandir Sahib

It is the place where Guru Hargobind had grown orchards and herbal plants. It was from his *shafakhana* here that Guru Har Rai sent the traditional medicines for Prince Dara Shikoh which cured his ailment. Later the prince came to thank the guru and stayed at this place.

Gurdwara Manji Sahib

Entrance to Gurdwara Manji Sahib at Kiratpur

This was the house of Bibi Rup Kaur (daughter of Guru Har Rai). In this gurdwara there are relics like a handmade handkerchief of Bibi Rup Kaur, a handwritten manuscript of the sacred scripture of that time, a handfan of Bibi Rup Kaur, Baba Sri Chand's *topi* (that was gifted to Baba Gurditta and Mata Basi gave it to Bibi Rup Kaur in dowry). The old historic building has recently been demolished to construct a new gurdwara.

Gurdwara Patalpuri

This gurdwara is situated on the banks of the river Sutlej. Last rites of Guru Hargobind and Guru Har Rai were performed here. The mortal remains of Guru Har Krishan were also brought from Delhi and immersed here. Most of the Sikhs carry the mortal remains of their relatives for immersion at Patalpuri.

Gurdwara Bibangarh

The gurdwara marks the place where Guru Gobind Singh received the severed head of his father, Guru Tegh Bahadur, carried from Delhi by Bhai Jaita and his companions, Bhai Agahiya and Bhai Uda. The head was carried by the guru and the *sangat* to Anandpur Sahib and cremated at a place called Sis Ganj.

In addition to the above gurdwaras, forts and *baolis*, there are a number of old historic *havelis* where Sodhi descendants of the gurus used to live. There are also gurdwaras built in the memory of Baba Sri Chand, son of Guru Nanak, and Baba Gurditta, son of Guru Hargobind.

Below: Gurdwara Bhatta Sahib, Ropar

Far below: A decorated sword of Guru Gobind Singh at Gurdwara Bhatta Sahib

Below right: Gurdwara Patalpuri in Kiratpur

Tercentenary Celebrations

Celebration of the tercentenary of the creation of the Khalsa in 1999 was a major event in the recent history of Anandpur Sahib. A year-long celebration was launched on 8th April, 1999 with the Prime Minister of India, cabinet ministers, chief ministers of Panjab and other states along with important leaders paying homage to the Khalsa. On 13th April prominent Sikh personalities from different walks of life were honoured with *Nishan-e-Khalsa* at an impressive ceremony at Anandpur Sahib. On 14th April a conclave of spiritual leaders was also organised wherein religious leaders belonging to different faiths from all over the world reached Anandpur Sahib to pay their homage to the Khalsa. It is estimated that more than five million visitors from across the world visited Anandpur Sahib during the tercentenary celebrations. Singh Sahib Bhai Manjit Singh, the Jathedar of Kesgarh, launched a novel campaign for environmental protection by popularising the idea of saplings being offered as *prasad*. This attracted the attention of the media worldwide. The celebration also resulted in major improvement of roads and other means of transport. In preparation for the celebrations, the whole city, including the historic gurdwaras, was painted white.

Left: Millions of devotees converged at Anandpur during the tercentenary celebrations.
Photo: Bandeep Singh
Courtesy: India Today

Below: Decorated elephants attracted special attention during the tercentenary celebrations.
Photo: Bandeep Singh
Courtesy: India Today

Below right: Takhat Kesgarh Sahib which was the main centre of celebrations in 1999.

Following double spread: Sea of turbans of devotees at Anandpur

Page 90 top: Enthusiastic devotees from nearby villages waiting for the tercentenary procession.

Page 90 below: Guru Granth Sahib being carried in procession on a decorated elephant

Page 91 top: A year long tercentenary celebrations of the Khalsa were inaugurated at Anandpur Sahib where the Prime Minister and other important leaders of India paid tributes to Guru Gobind Singh and the Order of the Khalsa.
Photo: T.S. Bedi
Courtesy: India Today

Page 91 below: A conclave of spiritual leaders at Anandpur Sahib where a representative of His Holiness, the Pope and, leading Hindu, Muslim, Jewish, Jain and Buddhist leaders joined in paying tributes to the Khalsa

Left: Singh Sahib Prof. Manjit Singh, Jathedar, Takhat Kesgarh Sahib, offering saplings as prasad
Photo: T. S. Bedi
Courtesy: India Today

Below: In a survey conducted by The Hindustan Times, *Bhai Vir Singh* (AD 1872-1957), *eminent Panjabi littérateur, was voted as the Greatest Sikh of Twentieth Century and was honoured with Nishan-e-Khalsa*

Right: Citation

Far right top: Medal

Far right middle: Silver case

Far below: The Sikh Heritage Complex under construction at Anandpur Sahib

93

To commemorate this unique event, the Government of Panjab inaugurated the Sikh Heritage Complex in Anandpur Sahib designed by world famous Israeli architect, Moshe Safdie. Located in 18-acre area in the foots of Shivalik hills, the complex would have different wings displaying various aspects of history and religion of the Sikhs. The first wing would have an art gallery, library and an auditorium with a seating capacity of 450 and equipped with the latest technology. The second wing would house a multi-media gallery. A huge *khanda* has also been erected in one part of the compound, reminiscent of the unique event associated with Anandpur Sahib. Another wing would display relics connected with the Sikh gurus and manuscripts of *Guru Granth Sahib Birs*. To be completed at a cost of over 300 crore rupees, the complex will be ready by December, 2002.

Apart from Anandpur Sahib, tercentenary of the Khalsa was also celebrated in different parts of India and abroad, wherever there is noticeable presence of the Sikhs. Special functions were organised in England, the United States, Canada and Singapore. These celebrations have created a renewed sense of awareness and pride in the rich heritage of the Khalsa created at Anandpur Sahib in AD 1699.

Far above: Welcome arches constructed during the tercentenary celebrations leading to the city of Anandpur

Above: Existing roads were repaired and new roads were provided in preparation of the tercentenary celebrations.

Right: Gold and silver tokens were issued by the Government of Panjab to commemorate the tercentenary of the Khalsa.

Left: Tercentenary procession reaching Takhat Kesgarh Sahib
Photo: Bandeep Singh
Courtesy: India Today

Glossary

amrit: baptismal nectar also called pahul

bandook: gun

baoli: well

bhora: underground cell used for meditation

burcha: spear

burchee: small spear

charan pahul: nectar prepared with the touch of guru's toe

chola: cloak

dhuan: preaching centre

dumala: tailpiece of turban

farra: part of the turban left hanging

gurbani: hymns of the gurus

hukamnama: direction to the Sikhs from the guru or the Akal Takhat

janamsakhi: popular hagiographical account of the life of Guru Nanak

kamarkasa: waist-belt

katar: sword

keski: a small turban

khalifa: caliph

khanda: double-edged sword

khande ki pahul: nectar first prepared by Guru Gobind Singh with the double-edged sword to baptise the five beloved ones

kharawan: wooden slippers

kirpan: sword, one of the five symbols worn by the baptised Sikhs

langar: free community kitchen

mahants: hereditary custodians of a shrine

masands: representatives of the gurus responsible for collection of donations in their respective areas

misl: confederacy

neza: javelin

nihangs: nihangs, literally dragons, were a special squad of army created by Guru Gobind Singh.

pahul: nectar

panj piaras: five beloved ones; the term used by Guru Gobind Singh for the first five Sikhs who were initiated into the order of the Khalsa

panth: Sikh community

patasa: sweet bubbles made of sugar

prasadi haathi: a rare elephant with a mark like a pan-cake on its forehead

sangat: congregation

shafakhana: hospital providing traditional herbal medicines

tabalbaz: washing bowl

takhat: literally throne; seat of temporal authority in the Sikh context

takia: literally pillow; Muslim hermitage in this context

thali: metal plate

topi: headgear like a cap used by Baba Sri Chand

udasi: derived from udas, meaning dejected, is used for the followers of Baba Sri Chand. They are celibate sadhus with a peculiar dress.